Totally Gross Chemistry

Peter Rillero, Ph.D.
Illustrator: Rémy Simard

PUBLICATIONS INTERNATIONAL, LTD.

Peter Rillero, Ph.D., is an assistant professor of science education at Arizona State University West in Phoenix. He is the coauthor of *365 Science Projects and Activities* and is a consulting editor for the journal *Science Activities*. Rillero has taught high school science in New York City and Kenya, as well as college science in Costa Rica. As a Fulbright Scholar, he lectured in science education at the University of Akureyri in Iceland.

Computer Illustration: Rémy Simard

Working with chemicals can be a dangerous activity and can result in serious injury. Follow directions carefully, never substitute ingredients, and all children must be supervised by an adult. The publisher, authors, and consultants specifically disclaim liability for any loss or injury incurred as a consequence of the use and application, either directly or indirectly, of any advice or information presented herein.

Copyright © 1999 Publications International, Ltd.
All rights reserved. This book may not be reproduced or quoted in whole or in part by any means whatsoever without written permission from:

Louis Weber, C.E.O.
Publications International, Ltd.
7373 North Cicero Ave.
Lincolnwood, Illinois 60646

Permission is never granted for commercial purposes.

Manufactured in China.

8 7 6 5 4 3 2 1

ISBN: 0-7853-3582-X

Table of Contents

- 4   Ick-troduction
- 6   I'm Melting!!!
- 7   Chemical Poppers
- 8   Bugs Clean Pee
- 9   Attack of Killer Slime
- 10   Ghost Writer
- 11   Foam Machine
- 12   Bloody Current
- 14   It's Absorbing
- 15   Put Him on the Rack
- 16   Moo Glue
- 17   When Good Wine Goes Bad
- 18   Virtual Vomit
- 19   Spit Don't Quit
- 20   Creepy Crystals
- 21   Grody Corrody
- 22   Knotted Bones
- 23   Pseudo Snot
- 24   The Battle of Liver and Potato
- 25   Bleeding Red Cabbage
- 26   Do You Drink Acid?
- 27   Ooze
- 28   Yucky Yolk
- 29   Gloop
- 30   Racing Weird Color Changes
- 31   Erupting Color Flow
- 32   Glossary

Ick-troduction

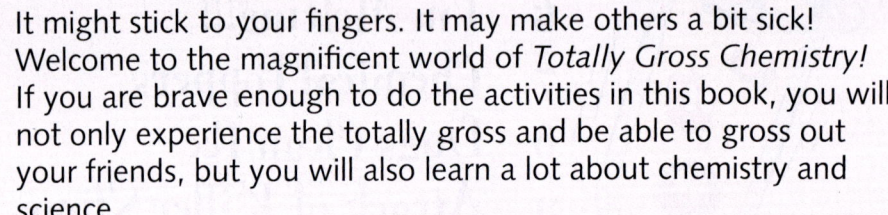

It might stick to your fingers. It may make others a bit sick! Welcome to the magnificent world of *Totally Gross Chemistry*! If you are brave enough to do the activities in this book, you will not only experience the totally gross and be able to gross out your friends, but you will also learn a lot about chemistry and science.

The Stuff of Chemistry

Chemistry is the study of stuff, and how this stuff interacts with other stuff. Chemists call stuff "matter." And, as a matter of fact, matter is made of molecules. The properties these molecules have make the world of the totally gross possible.

Important Stuff

While the world of gross and icky is totally cool, most chemists apply their work to other areas. Chemists may work to produce materials or methods to make food safer, to reduce pollution, to make people healthier, or to make our world more beautiful. Using chemistry to improve the lives of others and possibly to get fame and fortune is fine—if you're an adult! But hey, you're a kid. Sure, if you complete activities in this book you may choose to pursue a career in science, but that can wait. Let's get gross and icky first!

Sticky Details

Adult Permission: Suppose you take the next step; you turn some pages and find an activity that appeals to your gross side. What do you do? First read the activity so you understand what to do. Then show the activity to an adult and have them read it. Get adult permission to do the activity! There are many good reasons to do this.

1. Adults can help you to understand the steps of the activity.
2. Adults can help you gather materials for the activity.
3. Adults can celebrate your totally gross achievement.
4. Adults can help you understand what happened in the activity.
5. Adults can help clean up.
6. Adults can prevent accidents. Of course, adults can sometimes cause accidents, but ask yourself, which is worse, if you get Moo Glue on the new tablecloth or if your mom gets Moo Glue on it? You don't have to be a biochemist to figure that one out!

Safe Science: If you are not careful, far worse things than staining a tablecloth can happen. Whenever you work on an activity, practice safe science. If an activity says you should wear goggles, then you should definitely wear goggles! Your eyes are sensitive and important; protect them from chemicals. Another safe practice is to not eat or drink anything unless you are told it is okay. Also, don't leave things around where others might accidentally eat or drink them.

A lot of safe science is really common sense. For instance if you make something and it begins to get smelly, throw it away! This is totally gross chemistry, not stinky putrid chemistry. If it smells bad, it is probably because it is rotting—so pitch it. Some day you might grow into a top researcher, but for now don't invent your own experiments—follow the instructions. Also please remember—get adult permission before doing any activity! Some activities require that you have an adult help you do the activity. Never do these activities without an adult.

Seek Understanding: As you create a grosser and ickier world through chemistry, try to understand what is going on. Seek to know why an activity did what it did. Doing the experiment is a feat, but understanding the experiment is an even higher achievement. Read the explanations and the fun facts to help you learn more. Knowing a little will make you want to know more. Ask questions, read books, and learn more about chemistry. Facts are sticky—when you know some, others seem to stick right to them. The more you know, the more you will want to know. The more you know, the easier it is to know more.

Develop Skills: While facts are important in science, equally important is the ability to do science. Good scientists have many skills. One of the most important skills is the ability to make good observations. Be observant as you do the activities. Carefully watch what happens. Good scientists are also good experimenters; they observe what happens under different conditions. The totally gross experiments will help you to better understand experimentation and how scientists make conclusions from their experiments.

Conclusion

The totally gross world awaits you. Be brave. Be safe. Be observant. Seek understanding. Develop science skills. And by all means enjoy what you create and enjoy your observations of other people's reactions to your totally gross stuff. Seeing your art teacher's reaction to Virtual Vomit, your father play with Gloop, or your neighbor gross out to Pseudo Snot will help you appreciate how fun chemistry can be!

I'm Melting!!!

A witch placed into acetone melts into sticky goo. The goo can be molded into different shapes before it hardens.

What You'll Need

foam cup
pen
goggles
rubber gloves
acetone (nail polish remover)
glass or metal bowl

1. Draw a picture of a wicked witch on an upside-down foam cup. Put on the goggles and rubber gloves.

2. Pour acetone into the bowl so it is about ½ inch deep.

3. Put the witch into the acetone, feet first. Watch as the witch melts, just like the wicked witch in *The Wizard of Oz!* As you watch, say in your best witch voice, "I'm melting, I'm melting."

4. When the witch has totally melted, reach into the acetone and pull out the goo. (It looks like mucus, but it'**S NOT**!) Mold it into any shape—when it dries you will have a statue.

Safety

Adult supervision is needed for this project. Protect your eyes from the acetone by wearing goggles and your hands by wearing rubber gloves. Don't pour the acetone into a plastic bowl because it could damage the bowl. Do this activity in an area with good air circulation.

What Happened?

Similar to salt dissolving in water, polystyrene foam dissolves in acetone. The foam in the cup holds millions of tiny pockets of air. This makes the cup a great insulator, helping to keep your hot chocolate warm on cold days. When the foam dissolves in the acetone, the air is released, and a sticky goo results. When the foam goo hardens, it doesn't have air pockets anymore.

Fun Fact

Styrofoam is made from a chemical called polystyrene. The Dow Chemical Company invented it in the 1940s. Polystyrene beads are heated and air is blown in to create air bubbles in the foam. It is used for cups, home insulation, packing material, and flotation devices.

Chemical Poppers

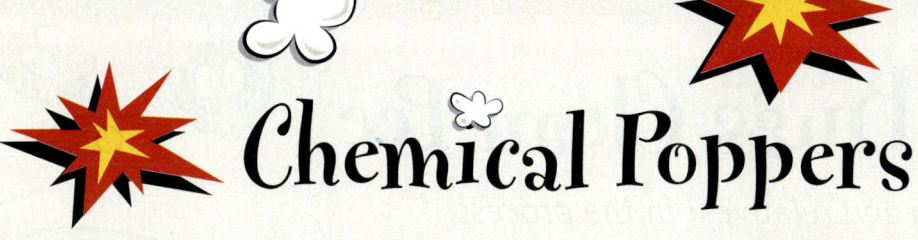

All you need to create an oozing mess and a loud pop are a film container and simple chemicals!

What You'll Need

facial tissue
teaspoon
baking soda
vinegar
plastic 35mm film container
goggles
spoon

1. Tear the tissue so you have a 4×4-inch square.

2. Put 1 teaspoon baking soda into the tissue square. Wrap it into a ball.

3. Put 3 teaspoons vinegar into the film container. Put on the goggles.

4. This part is tricky. Hold the lid of the film container in one hand. Put the baking soda wrapped in the tissue into the container. Quickly put on the lid. Make sure the lid is snapped shut all around.

5. Stand back and watch.

Safety

Adult supervision is needed for this project. Everybody nearby should wear goggles to protect eyes from the popping lid. Do this in the kitchen for easy clean-up.

What Happened?

When vinegar (acetic acid) is mixed with baking soda (sodium bicarbonate), it produces a chemical reaction. Carbon dioxide gas is produced. As more and more gas is produced, pressure in the film container builds, until POOF! The lid is blown off, revealing bubbling foam. It is important to have the lid completely snapped on or the carbon dioxide gas will sneak out the sides and the pressure will not build. Try varying the concentration of vinegar and baking soda until you have the perfect concentration that will allow you enough time to put the lid on, but still produce the loudest pop. If you are really fast at putting the lid on, try it without the tissue. You can put the baking soda directly into the vinegar. This produces a bigger pop and a more oozing mess.

Fun Fact

Vinegar is an acidic liquid made by microorganisms. Yeast changes sugar into alcohol. Bacteria turn the alcohol into vinegar. If wine gets too old, it turns into vinegar.

Bugs Clean Pee

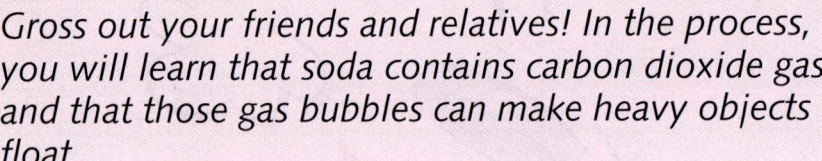

Gross out your friends and relatives! In the process, you will learn that soda contains carbon dioxide gas and that those gas bubbles can make heavy objects float.

What You'll Need

raisins
small bowl that looks scientific
tablespoon
water
beaker or tall glass
yellow soda

1. Put 4 to 6 raisins in a bowl with 1 tablespoon water. The raisins will absorb some water and look more like bugs.

2. Pour the yellow soda into the glass. Hide the soda bottle and the raisin box.

3. Gather your audience. Hold up the glass with the yellow soda and tell them this is pee. Feel free to use the scientific name, "urine."

4. Hold up the raisins in the bowl and tell them they are bugs that have been genetically engineered to get their food from pee and to clean the pee. The scientists who engineered the bugs named them *Bugus urinalis*, but that their nickname is Pee Pals. Explain that the Pee Pals are a little sluggish until they eat.

5. Drop the Pee Pals into the glass, and they will sink to the bottom. Explain that the bugs are now eating. After a short time some will rise to the top of the surface and then fall back down. They keep repeating this "dance." Explain to the audience that the Pee Pals rise to the top to get oxygen and then fall back down to the bottom to clean the urine.

6. After a few minutes announce in a dramatic way, "The Pee Pals have cleaned the urine!" Ask for volunteers to drink it. When everybody says, "No way," you dramatically drink the beverage. Then tell everybody how good it tastes.

Safety

In this activity you drink soda that you pretend is urine. Of course, you should never drink real urine! Don't drink or eat things you make in chemistry.

What Happened?

The raisins sink to the bottom of the glass of soda because they are denser than the soda. The fizz (or carbonation) of soda is from the carbon dioxide gas it contains. Carbon dioxide bubbles attach to the raisins, and the raisins rise. At the surface the bubbles are released, and the raisins sink back down.

Attack of Killer Slime

Create a slime chamber to attack a toy soldier! In the process you will learn about viscosity.

What You'll Need
2 baby food jars with lids
strong glue
small plastic toy soldier
goggles
drill with ¼-inch drill bit
light corn syrup
green food coloring
spoon

1. Glue the baby food jars back to back. Glue the plastic soldier to the inside bottom of one baby food jar. Allow the glue to dry.

2. Put on the goggles. Have an adult help you drill a hole through the 2 lids.

3. Fill the jar without the soldier with corn syrup. Stir in green food coloring until you have the perfect shade of green for your slime.

4. Screw the attached lids onto the jar with green slime; then screw the jar with the soldier onto the other side of the lid.

5. Flip the jars so the soldier is standing up. The slime will flow from the top jar to the bottom jar to cover the soldier. Flip over the jars for the slime to return to the first jar.

6. Find the Slime Time—how long does it take for the slime to flow from jar to jar? Put the jars in the refrigerator for 30 minutes to see if temperature affects Slime Time.

Safety
Adult supervision is needed for the gluing and drilling. Wear goggles when you drill.

What Happened?
The corn syrup flows slowly through the hole. One chemical property of liquids is their viscosity. The corn syrup has a high viscosity, so it flows slowly.

Fun Fact
Viscosity is the resistance to flow of a liquid. The motor oil in cars is very viscous. It sticks to the metal parts and prevents wear and tear due to friction.

Ghost Writer

Write a ghostly message! It is invisible until it's warmed.

What You'll Need
lemon
small bowl
toothpick
paper
lamp with lightbulb

1. Squeeze the juice of a lemon into a small bowl.

2. Using a toothpick as a pen and the lemon juice as ink, write something a ghost might say on a sheet of paper.

3. Show the note to a friend. When they can't read it, tell them it is because it was written by a ghost. Since ghosts are cold, the only way to read the note is to make it warm.

4. Hold the note near a lightbulb that is on. As the lightbulb warms the paper, the writing is revealed.

Safety
Adult supervision is needed for this project. Do not touch the lightbulb—it is very hot! Do not hold the paper too close to the bulb—you don't want it to catch on fire.

What Happened?
The lemon juice is an acid. It reacts very slowly with the cellulose in paper to make the paper brown. Ordinarily the reaction might take a few weeks to happen. When you add heat, however, the reaction speeds up. So you'll see the writing quickly when you hold the paper up to the heat.

Fun Fact
Many chemical reactions need heat to start them and keep them going. Some reactions may proceed without heat, but the presence of heat speeds up the reactions.

Foam Machine

Being a mad chemist has never been so easy. Create a foaming chemical reaction to prove your genius!

What You'll Need

goggles
2 test tubes (or similar shaped glasses)
powdered laundry detergent
teaspoon
vinegar
2 coffee stirrers
baking soda
water

1. Put on the goggles. Place ½ teaspoon powdered laundry detergent into test tube A. Fill it a ⅓ of the way with vinegar. Stir gently.

2. Place ½ teaspoon baking soda into test tube B. Fill it a ⅓ with water. Stir.

3. Pour the contents of test tube B into test tube A.

4. Check it out! Watch the foam as it oozes and oozes all over the place.

Safety

Wear goggles while doing this activity. And be sure to do this activity over a covered area or the sink—we don't want Mom or Dad unhappy!

What Happened?

The acidic vinegar and the alkaline baking soda (sodium bicarbonate) produce a chemical reaction. Carbon dioxide is produced by the reaction. It combines with the soap to produce foam that oozes out of the test tube.

Fun Fact

Baking soda is made of a chemical called sodium bicarbonate. This chemical occurs in all living things. It helps keep the pH of organisms in balance. The pH scale tells us if a solution is acid or alkaline. A pH of 1 is very acidic and 6 is slightly acidic. A pH of 7 is neutral; distilled water has a pH of 7. A pH of 8 is slightly alkaline and 14 is very alkaline.

Bloody Current

This spooky trick will amaze your friends and teach them about ions and electricity.

What You'll Need

2 bowls
measuring spoons
salt
red food coloring
water
small bowl
flashlight bulb and bulb holder
2 D batteries
3 insulated wires (about 5 to 7 inches long), stripped at both ends (ask a parent for help)
tape
mixing spoon

1. Place about 5 teaspoons salt in one bowl. Put 6 drops red food coloring into 1 tablespoon water in another bowl, and pour it over the salt. Mix.

2. Set up the electric circuit by referring to the diagram and steps below.

3. Attach wire A and wire B to the two terminals of the lightbulb holder (with lightbulb attached).

4. Tape the free end of wire B to the top of the batteries.

5. Tape wire C to the bottom of the batteries. Be sure batteries are touching each other.

6. Test your circuit by touching the free ends of wire A with wire C, which should cause the bulb to light. If not, fix your circuit, then go on.

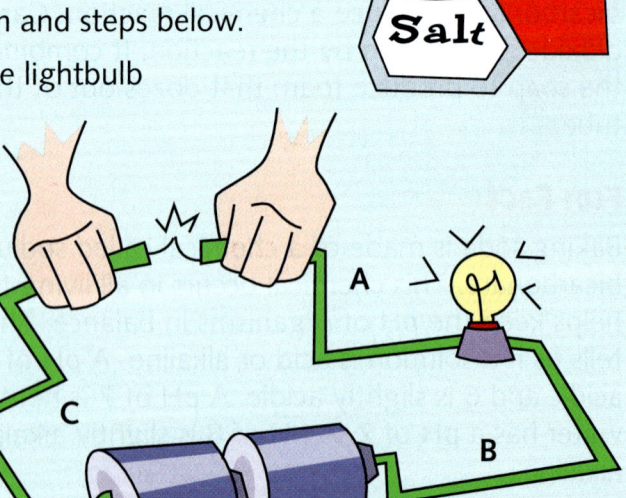

7. Bend the free ends of wires B and C over a bowl so the wires will be in the water.

8. Fill the small bowl with water until the wires are well below the surface of the water. The lightbulb should not light because water is a poor conductor of electricity.

9. Now have friends come over. Show them the setup, and have them observe the lightbulb. Ask them if they know who Frankenstein's monster was. The monster was "born" when electricity brought him to life. Show them the red salt, and tell them it is dried monster blood.

10. Pour the red salt into the water, and stir it. As the salt dissolves the light comes on!

Safety

Adult supervision is needed for this project. The circuit will not put out enough electricity to cause harmful shocks, but if the wires are connected incorrectly they may get hot because of a short circuit. If so, disconnect the circuit, and make sure wires only touch what they should.

What Happened?

Water is a poor conductor of electricity. When the table salt (sodium chloride) is poured into the water, the positive sodium ions separate from the negative chloride ions. These ions conduct electricity, and the light turns on.

Fun Fact

Batteries supply electricity because of the chemicals they contain. One part of the battery contains positive ions and the other part contains negative ions. When the circuit is connected, electrons flow through a wire from the negative part of the battery to the positive part of the battery.

It's Absorbing

Study the water absorbing ability of Super Absorbing Polymer; then use your knowledge in an impressive magic trick.

What You'll Need

goggles
2 disposable diapers
scissors
dark sheet of paper
2 foam cups
graduated cylinder or small measuring cup
water

1. Put on the goggles. Cut open the part of a clean diaper that absorbs the baby's urine.

2. Gently run your fingers over the cotton surface, and let the powder and crystals fall onto a dark sheet of paper. You now have Super Absorbing Polymer. Don't rub your fingers too roughly over the diaper surface, you want the crystals, not the cotton.

3. Put the Super Absorbing Polymer into the bottom of a foam cup.

4. How much water does the Polymer hold? Measure 2 milliliters of water, and pour it in. Keep doing this until the Polymer doesn't hold any more water. Calculate the total amount of water the Super Absorbing Polymer from one diaper holds.

5. Now here's the really cool part. Repeat the above procedures so you have the dry Super Absorbing Polymer in the foam cup. Stand in front of your friends and family without letting them know you have anything in the cup. Take an amount of water the Super Absorbing Polymer can easily hold and slowly and dramatically pour it into the cup. Talk for a minute while the water is being absorbed. Then dramatically turn the cup upside down. To the amazement of all, NOTHING COMES OUT. You can call it magic, or you can ask them to guess how you did it.

Safety

Adult supervision is needed for this activity. The Super Absorbing Polymer can be harmful if swallowed. It can cause drying and irritation of the eyes and inner nose. Wear goggles when you use this material. Even though you did careful measuring, it's a good idea not to turn the cup of water upside down over something that could be damaged by water.

What Happened?

The chemical name for Super Absorbing Polymer is sodium polyacrylate. Its chemical structure allows it to absorb a lot of liquid. Now you know why it is used in diapers!

Fun Fact

Polymers, such as Super Absorbing Polymer and nylon, are very long molecules. Much like a tower of blocks, a polymer is made of a simple molecule that gets joined into long chains.

Put Him on the Rack

In medieval days, they would put people on the rack and stretch them out. Use chromatography to stretch out a person drawn with a black marker—it's fun and no one gets hurt!

What You'll Need

paper coffee filter
scissors
black water-soluble marker
glass
water

1. Cut a 1×4-inch strip of coffee filter paper.

2. One inch above the bottom of the strip, draw a person with the marker.

3. Hang the strip over the side of a glass so the drawing is in the glass.

4. Add water to the glass so that only the 1 inch below the person is in the water. The drawing of the person should be above the water layer.

5. Watch what happens.

What Happened?

The water rises up the filter paper and dissolves the ink from the marker. The water carries this ink up the filter paper, and the person stretches. As the water moves up the filter paper, colors appear as the ink is separated. You might have thought black ink was just black ink, but actually black ink is made of several colors.

Fun Fact

Chromatography is used in chemistry to separate chemicals. For example, the green pigments of plants can be separated with alcohol and filter paper. The reason for the separation of colors in chromatography is that different chemicals dissolve at different rates and adhere with different amounts of force. Much can be learned by testing with chromatography.

Moo Glue

Put stickiness to use! In this activity you will make useful glue from milk.

What You'll Need

- goggles
- skim milk
- measuring cup
- saucepan
- vinegar
- teaspoon
- tea strainer or cheesecloth
- baking soda
- water
- tablespoon
- glass
- borax
- mixing spoon
- paper

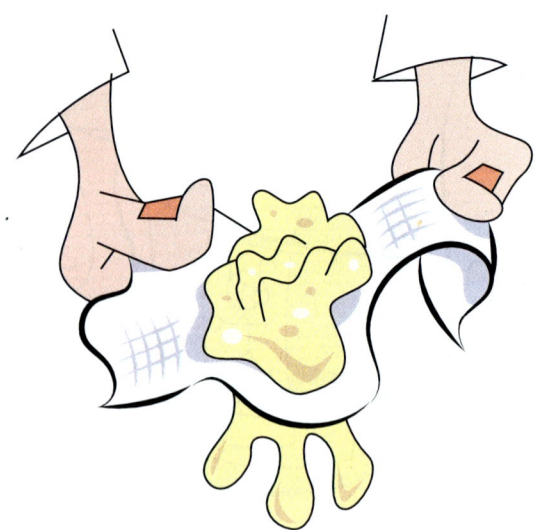

1. Put on the goggles. Warm 1 cup skim milk on a stove. (Don't heat milk to a boil.)

2. Stir in 2 teaspoons vinegar. The milk should separate into solid chunks.

3. Filter the chunks using a metal tea strainer or cheesecloth. Rinse the chunks with water to wash off all the acidic vinegar.

4. Sprinkle 1 teaspoon baking soda on top of the chunks to neutralize any remaining acid.

5. Put 2 tablespoons warm water in a glass. Add ½ teaspoon borax. Stir and dissolve the borax as much as possible.

6. Add the chunks of milk to the glass with the borax solution. Let stand overnight. Now your glue is ready. Try it out on some sheets of paper.

Safety

Adult supervision is needed when using the stove. Wear goggles throughout the entire activity. Use the glue for a few days, and then discard unused glue.

What Happened?

When the acidic vinegar is added to the warm milk, it causes the milk to curdle. The protein in the milk unravels and forms new connections. When proteins change shape like this, chemists say they have become denatured. The borax causes the long protein strands to form chemical bonds between them, which makes the solution sticky. This results in white glue. Now you know why there is a cow on the Elmer's Glue label.

Fun Fact

It's hard to imagine life without Elmer's Glue All. It has been around for over 50 years—the Borden company started selling the white glue in 1947. It was a powder that had to be mixed with water. It cost 29 cents for 2 ounces.

When Good Wine Goes Bad

Make people think you turned good wine into bad wine—then surprise everyone when you turn it back into good wine! Use a pH sensitive liquid to do the magic trick.

What You'll Need

3 wine glasses
goggles
rubber gloves
measuring cup and spoons
vinegar
ammonia
water
red grape juice

1. Set up the 3 wine glasses. Put on the goggles and rubber gloves. Add ½ teaspoon vinegar to the third glass.

2. Add ⅛ teaspoon ammonia (this is a couple of drops) to the second glass.

3. Add ⅓ cup water to the first glass. Add 1 teaspoon red grape juice to this glass.

4. Here is the magic. Don't let the audience know there is anything in glasses 2 or 3. Hold up the first glass and say, "We start with wine." Pour the liquid from the first glass into glass 2. The solution will become green. Say, "Good wine has now gone bad."

5. Now ask the audience to hope real hard that the bad wine will become good wine again. Pour the liquid from glass 2 to glass 3. The pale red solution returns. Announce that the good wine has returned.

Safety

Adult supervision is needed for this activity. Wear goggles and rubber gloves when working with ammonia. Avoid skin contact with ammonia. If ammonia gets on your skin, wash immediately with lots of water. Clean wine glasses well after use. Don't let anybody drink from the wine glasses until they have been cleaned well with lots of water! Never eat or drink your chemistry experiments!

What Happened?

Grape juice changes color when it is combined with alkaline substances. The solution is pinkish in glass 1 because the pH of water is close to neutral. When poured into glass 2, it turns greenish because the ammonia creates an alkaline solution. When poured into glass 3, the acidic vinegar neutralizes the alkaline solution, and the solution becomes pinkish again.

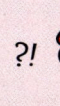

Virtual Vomit

Use kitchen stuff to unleash ultra-icky Virtual Vomit!

What You'll Need

saucepan
measuring spoons
oatmeal
water
measuring cup
applesauce
1 packet gelatin
powdered cocoa
breakfast cereal flakes
Teflon frying pan
wooden spoon
plastic spatula

1. Place 1 teaspoon oatmeal and 2 tablespoons water into a saucepan. Turn heat on low. Heat for 2 minutes.

2. Stir ⅓ cup applesauce into the saucepan. Add 1 packet gelatin. Add ⅓ teaspoon powdered cocoa. Add about 10 broken-up cereal flakes.

3. Stir a few times, but it is best to have it be a bit lumpy. Turn off heat, and allow it to cool for a few minutes. Pour mixture into a Teflon frying pan. With a wooden spoon, shape it into the desired vomit shape. Allow it to cool completely.

4. Use a plastic spatula to lift the Virtual Vomit out of the pan, and place it on a plastic table, countertop, or concrete sidewalk where it will gross out somebody. Watch people's reactions as they see this super-icky solution!

Safety

Adult supervision is needed when working with the stove. Be careful where you place the Virtual Vomit—it could stain cloth or wood surfaces. If the Vomit is placed in a warm place, the gelatin may melt.

What Happened?

The water in the applesauce and the water you added dissolved the powdered gelatin. The solution was created with the addition of the heat. When the heat was removed, the solution cooled, and the gelatin formed into a solid.

Fun Fact

What is gelatin? It is the most important ingredient in the shaky stuff of Jell-O. Gelatin is made up of long protein strands. Most gelatins are made from cow and pig bones and skin.

Spit Don't Quit

Mom might have told you no spitting when you were little, but now you get to spit and learn something about enzymes at the same time. Chemistry is so cool!

What You'll Need

goggles
plate
cornstarch
iodine (available from drugstores)
2 test tubes (or similar shaped glasses)
bowl
2 coffee stirrers

1. Put on the goggles. Place a pinch of cornstarch on the plate. Add a drop of iodine. Notice the blue-black color produced. When iodine turns this color, it shows that starch is present.

2. Put 2 milliliters water into test tube A.

3. Gather your spit. Put 2 milliliters spit into test tube B. Spit gathering is easier if you think about lemons.

4. Mix 1/10 teaspoon cornstarch into each solution. Stir with the coffee stirrers (be sure to use a different stirrer for each test tube).

5. Place tubes in a warm place. Stir each test tube every 5 minutes. After 20 minutes, go on to the next step.

6. Add 2 drops of iodine to each test tube. Compare the test tubes. Record your observations.

Safety

Adult supervision is needed for this activity. Wear goggles when using iodine. Iodine will stain skin, along with clothes, tables, and countertops—be careful! Spit may contain germs, so don't touch someone else's spit. Wash your hands after collecting spit and after cleaning up.

What Happened?

Test tube A turns a blue-black color while test tube B has a smaller color change. This shows that test tube A has more starch than test tube B. The reason for this is the spit, also known as saliva, contains the enzyme salivary amylase that digests starch into sugars—so there is less starch in test tube B.

Fun Fact

The iodine in this experiment is a chemical indicator: It changed color in the presence of starch. Other chemicals are used to show the presence of other substances. For example, Benedict's solution shows the presence of simple sugars.

Creepy Crystals

Grow creeping crystals from a super-saturated solution! The mad scientist in you is emerging—beware science world!

What You'll Need

saucepan
Epsom salts
green food coloring
metal bottle caps
string
pennies

1. Heat ½ cup water in a saucepan. Use medium heat.

2. Stir in ½ cup Epsom salts. Turn off stove.

3. Add 2 drops green food coloring, and stir. Let mixture cool for 20 minutes or more.

4. Arrange the bottle caps in a pan. Carefully pour the warm solution into the bottle caps until the caps are full.

5. Place strings in the caps to observe crystals growing. Use pennies to weigh down the strings so they don't float.

6. Place the pan where the water will evaporate quickly. Warm areas with good airflow increase evaporation. Watch caps for a few weeks for crystal growth. If a crust forms on the top, use a pencil to make a hole so you can watch the crystals form.

Safety

Adult assistance is required when using the stove. Avoid burns; be careful as you pour the warm salt solution. Don't pour the salt solution onto a wooden surface because it could cause damage.

What Happened?

Epsom salts (magnesium dioxide) dissolve in water. Heating the water lets you dissolve more salt into the water. When you do this, you create what chemists call a super-saturated solution. After the water is poured into the caps, it begins to cool. Now the water can't hold as much salt, and crystals begin to grow. As the water evaporates, the crystals continue to grow.

Fun Fact

Look closely and compare a few grains of table salt and Epsom salt. You can see the crystals are different shapes. When large crystals grow, they are made out of the same repeated shapes.

Grody Corrody

Rust, muck, yuck! Your father hates when it happens to his car. What is needed to create corrosion?

What You'll Need
scissors
steel wool
3 test tubes

1. Cut 3 small equal-size pieces of steel wool, and place a piece into each test tube.

2. Don't add anything else to test tube 1.

3. In test tube 2, add enough water to totally submerge the steel wool.

4. In test tube 3, add enough water to submerge half the steel wool.

5. Leave test tubes for a few days, and observe the results.

Safety
An adult should cut the steel wool. Be careful to avoid splinters when handling the steel wool.

What Happened?
Only the steel wool in test tube 3 had rust. This is because both water and oxygen are needed for this chemical reaction to occur.

Fun Fact
The rusting of iron is a type of chemical reaction known as oxidation. Molecules of iron combine with molecules of oxygen to form rust molecules (ferric oxide).

Knotted Bones

Look Ma, I'm knotty!

This is chemistry with a twist!

What You'll Need
goggles
long, thin bone from a cooked chicken or turkey
tall glass
vinegar
plastic wrap

1. Put on the goggles. Place bone into a tall glass filled with vinegar.

2. Cover the glass with plastic wrap so your home won't smell like a pickle factory.

3. Observe the bone. Leave the bone for 3 days, then remove it from the vinegar. Notice how flexible the bone has become. If it is really flexible, proceed to the next step. Otherwise, pour out the old vinegar, and fill the glass with new vinegar. Leave the bone for a few more days.

4. Tie the bone into a knot. Allow it to dry. Show this to your friends, and see if they can explain how it happened.

Safety
Wear goggles to avoid getting vinegar in your eyes.

What Happened?
The vinegar (acetic acid) dissolved the calcium in the bone. Calcium makes bones hard and strong. Without the calcium, the bones became rubbery and flexible.

Fun Fact
Bones contain four minerals to make them strong: calcium, phosphorous, magnesium, and manganese. Of these minerals, calcium is the most important. Calcium is found in milk, cheese, and green leafy vegetables.

Pseudo Snot

Here's your chance to use chemistry to gross out your family and friends!

What You'll Need

goggles
borax
measuring cup and spoons
3 small cups
yellow (or green) food coloring
white glue
mixing spoon

1. Put on the goggles. Dissolve ½ teaspoon borax into ¼ cup water in one cup.
2. Add 1 drop yellow food coloring to 3 teaspoons water in another cup.
3. Put 1 teaspoon white glue into the third cup.
4. Stir ½ teaspoon yellow water into glue.
5. Pour 1 teaspoon of the borax solution over the glue. Don't stir!
6. Put your fingers into the center of the solution and pull out a nice long strand of pseudo snot. Go into a room of people and pretend to sneeze, and hold the pseudo snot near your nose. Yuck! You have enough borax solution and yellow water to repeat this 5 more times. Experiment with different colors to find the perfect snot color.

Safety

Wear goggles when making the borax solution. Don't leave the borax solution in a place where someone might drink it. It might seem obvious, but DON'T eat the pseudo snot. Don't put pseudo snot in sinks or drains because it could cause clogs.

What Happened?

White glue is made of long strands of proteins. The borax causes these long strands to bond together tighter, so when you pull it up it looks like a long strand of snot. If you stir the pseudo snot, the long strands form a ball.

Fun Fact

Real snot is also made of protein chains. Real snot is called mucus—a real-life gross substance. Mucus is important because it captures the dust and dirt that you breathe in. It can also help fight germs that enter your body. Mucus is a great friend to your body. So if somebody calls you a real snot, say "Thanks!"

The Battle of Liver and Potato

Bubbles, bubbles, bubbles! Which can produce the most—liver or potato? This dandy experiment will show you.

What You'll Need
potato
liver
knife
cutting board
goggles
hydrogen peroxide (3% solution)
2 test tubes (or similar shaped glasses)
dish soap
mixing spoon
ruler
paper and pencil

1. Cut small, equal-size pieces of raw liver and potato. Put on the goggles.

2. Pour about 1 inch hydrogen peroxide solution into 2 test tubes or similarly shaped glasses.

3. Add 1 drop dish soap to each test tube, and stir gently.

4. Place a piece of liver in one test tube and a piece of potato in the other at the same time. Observe which produces the most bubbles.

5. Record the maximum heights of the foam columns in each test tube.

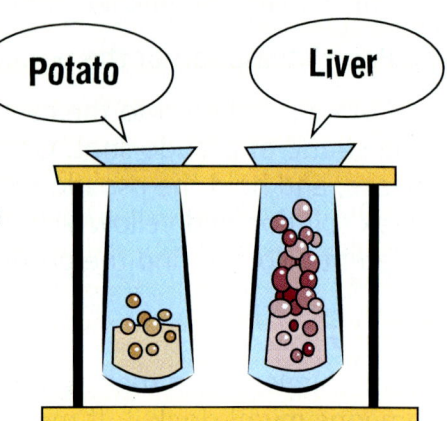

Safety
Adult supervision is needed for this activity. Be careful with sharp knives. Wash hands after handling liver. Do not drink hydrogen peroxide; wear goggles to avoid getting hydrogen peroxide in your eyes.

What Happened?
Dropping pieces of liver and potato into the hydrogen peroxide results in bubbling as oxygen is released. The interaction of the bubbles with the soap solution produces a good amount of foam. Liver produces more bubbles and foam than the potato. Liver wins because it has a greater amount of catalase—the enzyme that breaks down hydrogen peroxide.

Fun Fact
Enzymes are chemicals made by living things. They speed up, or catalyze, chemical reactions. Enzymes control everything your body does.

Bleeding Red Cabbage

Cabbage isn't just for St. Patrick's Day anymore—use it for exciting experiments!

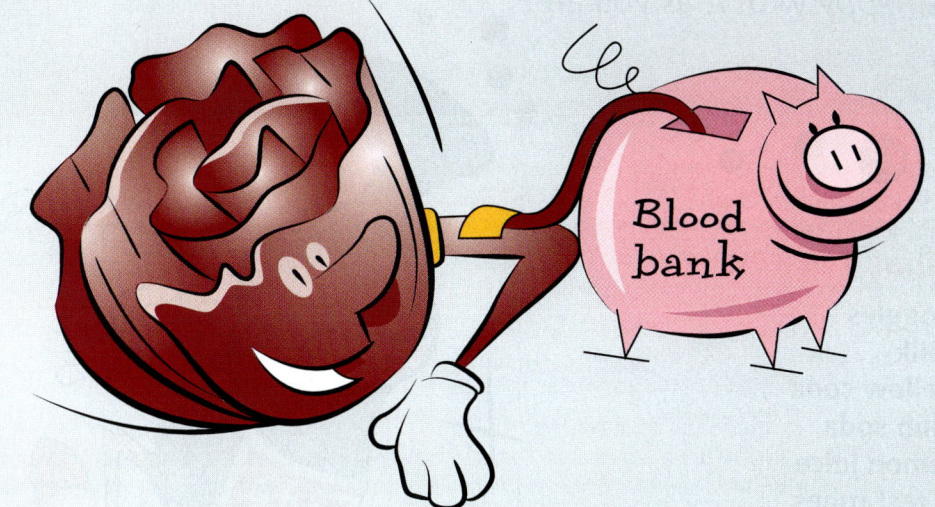

What You'll Need

¼ head red cabbage
measuring cup
saucepan
pot
strainer
funnel
glass bottle with cap
goggles
3 test tubes or glasses
rubber gloves
vinegar
ammonia

1. Cut cabbage into chunks. Put cabbage into a saucepan with 2 cups water. Heat to a low boil on the stove. Turn off the heat, and let water cool.

2. Place a strainer over the pot. Pour the cabbage juice into the strainer. Using a funnel, pour the cabbage juice into a bottle with a cap. Throw away the cabbage. You have made cabbage juice indicator.

3. Test your cabbage juice indicator. Put on the goggles and rubber gloves. Put a little indicator into 3 test tubes or glasses. Add an equal volume of water to dilute the indicator.

4. Add a few drops of vinegar to one test tube. Add a few drops of ammonia to the second test tube. Add a few drops of water to the third test tube.

5. Compare the color in each test tube. Keep your cabbage indicator for other experiments.

Safety

Adult supervision is needed for this activity. Wear goggles and rubber gloves when using the ammonia and vinegar. Avoid skin contact with the ammonia. If ammonia gets on the skin, wash immediately with lots of water.

What Happened?

Boiling the cabbage allowed its colored pigment to escape into the water. This pigment is pH sensitive. So when you added vinegar, it turned reddish. The cabbage indicator turns red in acidic solutions. When you added ammonia, it turned greenish. The cabbage indicator turns green in an alkaline solution.

Do You Drink Acid?

You may think your favorite soda is your friend—but guess what? Your teeth aren't as happy with it as you are!

What You'll Need

goggles
milk
yellow soda
club soda
lemon juice
4 test tubes
pH indicator strips or
 cabbage juice indicator
 (see page 25)
eyedropper

1. Put on the goggles. Pour 1 milliliter each of milk, soda, club soda, and lemon juice into separate test tubes.

2. Find out if the liquids are acidic, neutral, or alkaline. Use pH paper or the cabbage juice indicator. If you use the cabbage indicator, dilute 1 part cabbage juice to 4 parts water.

3. Compare the color of the solutions to the pH indicator chart in the glossary.

4. Write down the pH of the solutions.

Safety

Wear goggles when using universal indicator.

What Happened?

Some liquids are acidic and others are alkaline. The milk is alkaline; it contains a lot of calcium. The soda and lemon juice are acidic, in part because both contain citric acid. Find the pH of other drinks.

Fun Fact

When you eat food, your stomach secretes hydrochloric acid, a very acidic substance. So for most people, slightly acidic drinks don't bother their stomachs. But acidic beverages, like soda, can be bad for your teeth. The acid can dissolve the calcium—that's bad because calcium keeps your teeth strong.

Ooze

Ooze would have made Isaac Newton scratch his head with amazement!

What You'll Need
plastic mixing bowl
water
measuring spoons and cups
cornstarch
mixing spoon

1. Pour 1 cup water into a plastic mixing bowl.

2. Measure 1½ cups cornstarch. Place 1 tablespoon cornstarch into the water, and mix it in. Keep adding cornstarch and mixing it in.

3. When your solution gets very difficult to stir, you have Ooze.

4. Scoop some up with your hand, and watch how it oozes back into the bowl.

5. Use your fist to punch the Ooze (don't hit it so hard that you hurt your hand). You might expect Ooze to fly everywhere—but it doesn't. This is a fun thing to do with a friend, because they jump back thinking the Ooze will fly.

Safety
Dispose of Ooze in a plastic bag in the trash. Don't pour it down a sink; it will clog pipes.

What Happened?
The cornstarch-water solution creates a special fluid. It behaves a little like a liquid and a little like a solid. These fluids are called non-Newtonian fluids.

Fun Fact
Isaac Newton described ideal fluids back in the 1700s. Since then, scientists have found that not all fluids are ideal. A non-Newtonian fluid behaves differently. Ooze behaves a bit like a liquid and a bit like a solid. Quicksand is another non-Newtonian fluid. If you are ever caught in quicksand, don't move quickly, but try to make your way slowly to the shore.

Yucky Yolk

Do you have an emulsifying personality? Let's find out!

What You'll Need

measuring cup
vegetable oil
teaspoon
vinegar
2 mixing bowls
mixing spoon
eggbeater
1 egg, separated

1. Add ½ cup vegetable oil to a mixing bowl. Mix in 1 teaspoon vinegar. Note what happens.
2. Use the eggbeater to mix the vinegar and oil. Stop mixing, and watch it for a few minutes. Note what happens. You have shown that vinegar and oil don't stay mixed.
3. To another mixing bowl, add 1 teaspoon vinegar and 1 egg yolk. Beat the egg mixture until it is good and sticky.
4. Add 1 cup oil and 2 teaspoons vinegar. Mix together with the eggbeater.
5. Observe. You have mixed oil and vinegar together.

Safety
Do not taste or eat anything you make in chemistry!

What Happened?
When you put oil and vinegar together, the vinegar sank to the bottom of the glass. When you mixed it, the vinegar broke into tiny drops and the solutions seemed to mix. But after a while the little drops of vinegar combined to form bigger drops. These drops slowly sank to the bottom, and the vinegar and oil separated. When you mixed in the egg yolk, you got the oil and vinegar to stay mixed. The yolk contains lecithin. The lecithin molecules surround the oil and prevent the oil molecules from coming together, so they stay in solution much longer. You have created mayonnaise. Of course, if it were real mayonnaise you would need to add mustard and salt.

Fun Fact
When two liquids do not mix, they are said to be immiscible. Chemicals that act like lecithin to mix immiscible liquids are called emulsifiers. Detergents are emulsifiers; they break up oil into smaller sizes so it can be more easily washed from clothes or dishes.

Gloop

Here's another recipe that would have confused Mr. Newton!

What You'll Need

borax
teaspoon
glass
measuring cup
water
mixing spoon
white glue
bowl

1. Mix 1 teaspoon borax with ⅓ cup warm tap water in a glass. Stir well.
2. Mix ⅙ cup white glue with ⅙ cup water in a bowl. Stir well.
3. Mix 3 to 4 teaspoons borax solution into the glue. Less borax makes a slightly stickier Gloop. When the Gloop gets thick, knead it with your hands.
4. Play with the Gloop, and discover its properties. Notice how far it can be stretched. Mold it into a ball. Put the ball in the center of your palm. Observe how the ball becomes a liquid and drips between your fingers.

Safety

Throw the Gloop away in the trash—not the sink—it could clog the drain. As with other chemistry activities, don't eat anything you make.

What Happened?

The borax causes the long protein strands in the white glue to bond with other protein strands. These long strands cling together and allow the Gloop to be stretched long distances. When molded into a ball, it stays that way for a short time, but then gravity pulls it down and it becomes a liquid. This is another example of a non-Newtonian fluid. It behaves a little like a solid and a little like a liquid.

Fun Fact

Borax is a type of rock made of boron, sodium, and oxygen. Most of the world's borax is mined in California's Mojave Desert. Borax is used as bleach because it is milder than chlorine bleaches.

Racing Weird Color Changes

Acid fighter to the rescue! Find out which antacid tablet is the best one. Your parents will thank you on taco night!

What You'll Need

goggles
measuring cups
red cabbage indicator (see
    page 25)
water
4 glasses
eyedropper
vinegar
2 different brands of antacid tablets
2 coffee stirrers

1. Put on the goggles. Dilute the cabbage indicator by adding ¼ cup cabbage juice to 2 cups water in a glass. Add a few drops vinegar until cabbage indicator has a reddish color.

2. Pour ¼ cup diluted cabbage indicator into each of 3 glasses.

3. Gather the different antacid tablets. Crush 2 tablets of each antacid (keep brands separate).

4. Place the crushed tablets of the first antacid into the first glass. Place crushed tablets of the other antacid into the second glass. Don't put anything into the third glass—this is the control.

5. Stir each glass the same amount every 5 minutes. After 40 minutes, compare the colors in the glasses. Which antacid caused the biggest change in color?

Safety

This activity should be done with adult supervision. Never use medicine without adult approval. Wear goggles when working with vinegar.

What Happened?

The vinegar causes the cabbage color to change to red. As the antacid tablets dissolve, they neutralize some of the acid. This causes slow color changes in the cabbage indicator. The solution with the biggest color change is the stronger antacid.

Fun Fact

Antacids work by absorbing the hydrogen ions that are released by acids. The antacids combine with the acid and produce salt and water. Most antacids contain calcium, magnesium, or aluminum.

Erupting Color Flow

Turn Mom or Dad into a mad scientist with this bubbling beaker!

Caution: Working with dry ice can be dangerous. Only adults should do this activity. Never touch dry ice. Avoid contact with all body parts and with clothes. Wear rubber gloves, and hold the ice with thick, folded paper.

What You'll Need

goggles
rubber gloves
apron
red cabbage indicator (see see page 25)
tall glass
ammonia
eyedropper
plastic tub
small piece of dry ice

1. Put on the goggles, rubber gloves, and apron. Dilute the cabbage indicator by adding ¼ cup cabbage juice to 2 cups water.

2. Slowly and carefully add 1 drop ammonia. This should be sufficient to make the solution slightly green. If not, add another drop. Don't add too much ammonia or you won't be able to see a color change.

3. Fill a tall glass ⅓ full of diluted greenish cabbage juice. Put the glass inside a plastic tub.

4. Use a thick, folded sheet of paper to put the small piece of dry ice into the glass. Stand back, and observe what happens.

Safety

This activity must be done by adults. Wear goggles, rubber gloves, and an apron throughout the entire activity. Do this demonstration in a well-ventilated area. Do not let ammonia touch skin; if it does, wash with plenty of water. Keep ammonia away from eyes.

What Happened?

When the dry ice is added to the water, it releases carbon dioxide gas. This process is called sublimation—a solid becoming a gas. This causes the white smoke. The carbon dioxide gas dissolves in water, making carbonic acid. This acid changes the pH of the solution, and a color change is observed.

Glossary

Acid: Substance with a pH in the range of 0 to 6. Acids give off hydrogen ions (H+) in solutions.

Alkaline: Substance with a pH in the range of 8 to 14. Alkaline substances give off hydroxide ions (OH-) in solution.

Base: Another word for an alkaline substance.

Catalyst: A molecule that is involved in a chemical reaction and not changed by the reaction. The catalyst speeds up the rate of reaction.

Chemical reaction: This happens when molecules come together to produce new molecules.

Chemistry: The branch of science that deals with properties and interactions of matter.

Chromatography: A technique to separate chemicals. Chromatography separates chemicals based on how easily they dissolve in a fluid and how much they tend to stick to a surface.

Concentration: This usually refers to the amount of a chemical dissolved in a fluid.

Density: Refers to the amount of matter in a certain volume. The formula for density is mass divided by volume.

Enzyme: This is a catalyst made by a living thing. (See *catalyst*.) Enzymes are proteins.

Fluids: Any liquid or gas. In fluids, molecules can flow past each other.

Gas: A state of matter where the molecules are wide apart. Gases tend to have low density and low viscosity.

Indicator: A chemical that can be used to show the presence of another chemical.

Liquid: A state of matter where the molecules are closer than a gas but farther apart than a solid.

Molecules: The smallest particles of a chemical that have the properties of that chemical.

pH scale: A measure of the acid or alkaline in a solution. The scale ranges from 0 to 14. Low numbers are acidic, high numbers are alkaline, and seven is neutral. The pH chart below is for use with a red cabbage indicator. This chart shows numbers from 1 to 12.

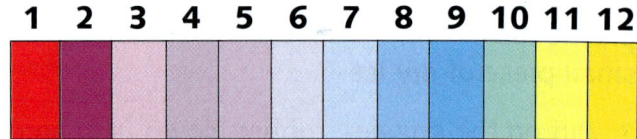

Polymer: A long molecule that is made by linking many small molecules into a chain. Protein and nylon are examples of polymers.

Protein: A long molecule made by linking together amino acids. The structures of many living things are made from proteins.

Solids: A state of matter where the molecules are close together and locked into position. Water becomes a solid when it is frozen.

Viscosity: This is a liquid's resistance to flow. All liquids have some viscosity.

Volume: The amount of space taken up by an object.